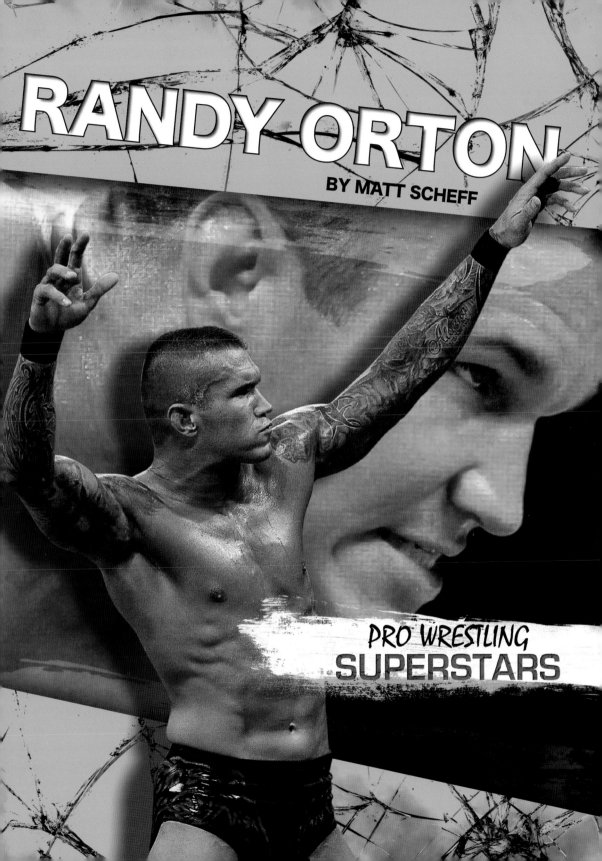

RANDY ORTON

BY MATT SCHEFF

PRO WRESTLING SUPERSTARS

Published by ABDO Publishing Company, PO Box 398166, Minneapolis, MN 55439. Copyright © 2014 by Abdo Consulting Group, Inc. International copyrights reserved in all countries. No part of this book may be reproduced in any form without written permission from the publisher. SportsZone™ is a trademark and logo of ABDO Publishing Company.

Printed in the United States of America,
North Mankato, Minnesota
082013
012014

Editor: Chrös McDougall
Series Designer: Jake Nordby

Photo Credits: Paul Abell/AP Images for WWE, cover, 1, 29 (inset), 30 (bottom); Mike Lano Photojournalism, cover (background), 1 (background), 7 (inset), 12, 13, 14-15, 30 (middle), 30 (top); Anna Ker/WP/MAXPPP/Newscom, 4-5; Matt Roberts/Zuma Press/Icon SMI, 6-7 , 18-19, 20-21, 26, 27, 31; Carrie Devorah/WENN Photos/Newscom, 8-9, 10-11, 22-23, 28-29; Stephane Allaman/ABACA/Newscom, 16-17; Titomedia/Splash News/Newscom, 24-25; SI1 WENN Photos/Newscom, 25 (inset)

Library of Congress Control Number: 2013945680

Cataloging-in-Publication Data

Scheff, Matt.
  Randy Orton / Matt Scheff.
    p. cm. -- (Pro wrestling superstars)
Includes index.
ISBN 978-1-62403-138-0
1. Orton, Randy--Juvenile literature. 2. Wrestlers--United States--Biography--Juvenile literature.   1. Title.
796.812092--dc23
[B]

                                                              2013945680

CONTENTS

THE WWE CHAMPIONSHIP

More than 16,000 fans screamed as Randy Orton and John Cena stepped into the steel cage in 2009. The bitter rivals were battling for the World Wrestling Entertainment (WWE) championship.

Cena was in control at first. But then Orton came on strong. He tied Cena's arms in the ropes. Then he put Cena into a choke hold. The referee stepped in and freed Cena from the ropes. But it was too late. Orton stepped up and kicked the champ in the head. Cena was out. Orton was the new WWE champion!

Randy Orton is one of WWE's biggest stars.

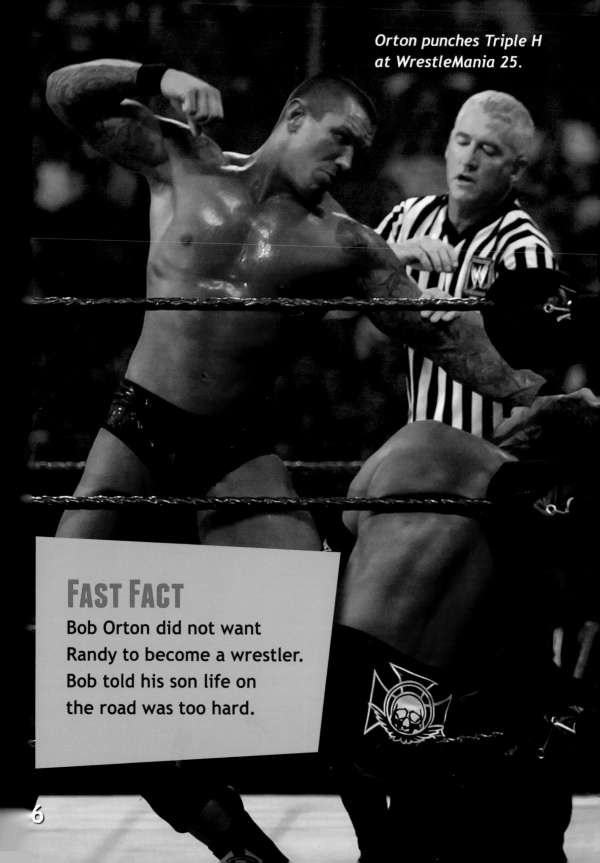

Orton punches Triple H at WrestleMania 25.

FAST FACT

Bob Orton did not want Randy to become a wrestler. Bob told his son life on the road was too hard.

THIRD-GENERATION WRESTLER

Randal Keith Orton was born April 1, 1980, in Knoxville, Tennessee. His father, "Cowboy" Bob Orton, was a professional wrestler. Randal's grandfather and uncle had also wrestled. Young Randy wanted to follow in their footsteps. He starred on his high school wrestling team.

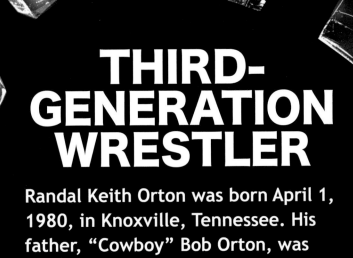

Orton in 2001

Orton is an intense wrestler.

Orton once had a Marine
Corps tattoo on his arm.
He has since had it covered
up with other tattoos.

Orton graduated from high
school in 1998. He enlisted in
the United States Marine Corps.
But life in the Marines was not
for Orton. He twice went absent
without leave (AWOL). That
meant he left his post without
permission. He also disobeyed
an officer's order. Orton was
punished for breaking Marine
Corps rules. He had to serve 38
days in a military prison.

BECOMING
A WRESTLER

Orton's military career was over.
So his father began training him to
wrestle. In 2000, Orton competed
in small independent wrestling
leagues. He also served as a
referee in his uncle's league,
World Organized Wrestling.

Orton wrestles against Primo in 2009.

Orton (front) *worked his way through the ranks before joining WWE.*

Orton poses for the fans.

WWE signed Orton to a
developmental contract
in 2001. He would have
to work his way up to the
big WWE events. Orton
started out in Ohio Valley
Wrestling (OVW). There,
he mastered the skills
he would need in WWE.
He won OVW's hardcore
championship twice.

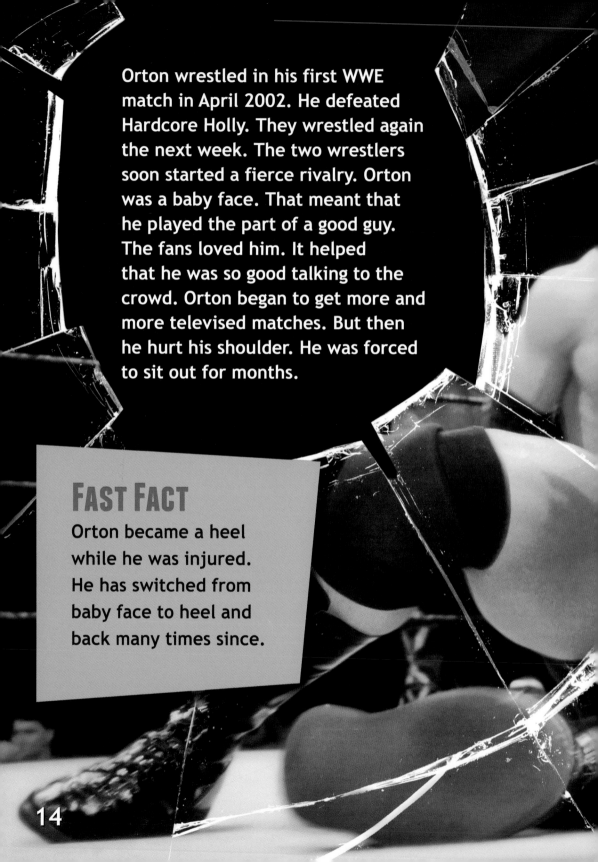

Orton wrestled in his first WWE match in April 2002. He defeated Hardcore Holly. They wrestled again the next week. The two wrestlers soon started a fierce rivalry. Orton was a baby face. That meant that he played the part of a good guy. The fans loved him. It helped that he was so good talking to the crowd. Orton began to get more and more televised matches. But then he hurt his shoulder. He was forced to sit out for months.

FAST FACT

Orton became a heel while he was injured. He has switched from baby face to heel and back many times since.

Orton feels the pain during his first year in WWE.

15

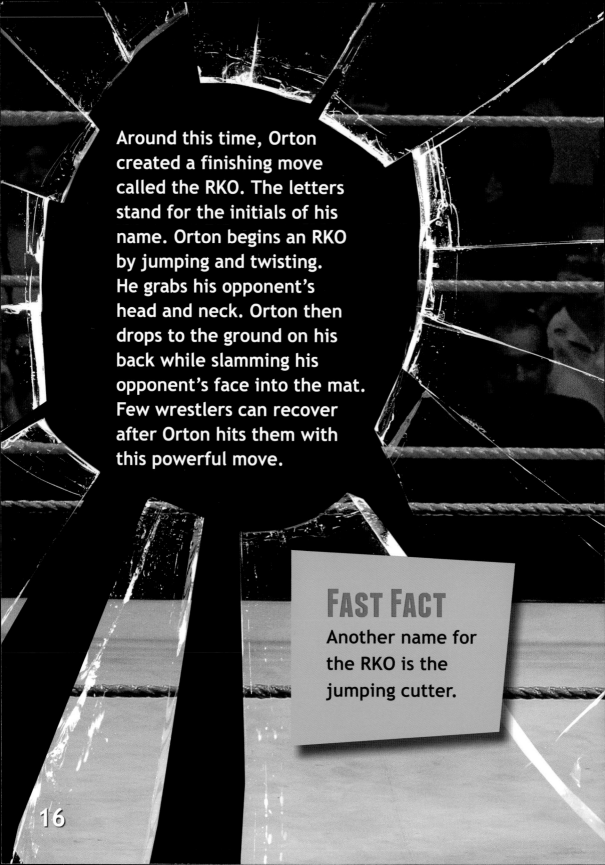

Around this time, Orton created a finishing move called the RKO. The letters stand for the initials of his name. Orton begins an RKO by jumping and twisting. He grabs his opponent's head and neck. Orton then drops to the ground on his back while slamming his opponent's face into the mat. Few wrestlers can recover after Orton hits them with this powerful move.

Fast Fact

Another name for the RKO is the jumping cutter.

Orton, right, *gets ready to drop Christian to the mat in 2011.*

THE LEGEND KILLER

Orton began calling himself "The Legend Killer." He wanted to beat all of WWE's greatest legends. He picked fights with WWE stars such as Shawn Michaels and Mick Foley.

In December 2003, Orton won his first title belt. He beat Rob Van Dam to claim the intercontinental championship. He held that title for seven months.

FAST FACT

Orton and Edge formed a tag team called Rated-RKO. They won the world tag-team championship in 2006.

Orton did not shy away from anyone in WWE.

Orton, right, faces down Triple H at WrestleMania 25.

In 2004, Orton faced Chris Benoit for the world heavyweight championship. Orton used an RKO to knock out the champ and win the belt.

John Cena later became WWE champion in 2007. However, WWE boss Vince McMahon stripped Cena of his belt. WWE awarded the title to Orton. Orton tried to defend it, but he lost to Triple H. Yet later that same night, he won it back. No one had ever claimed the same belt twice in a single night!

FAST FACT

At the age of 24, Orton was the youngest wrestler to win the world heavyweight championship.

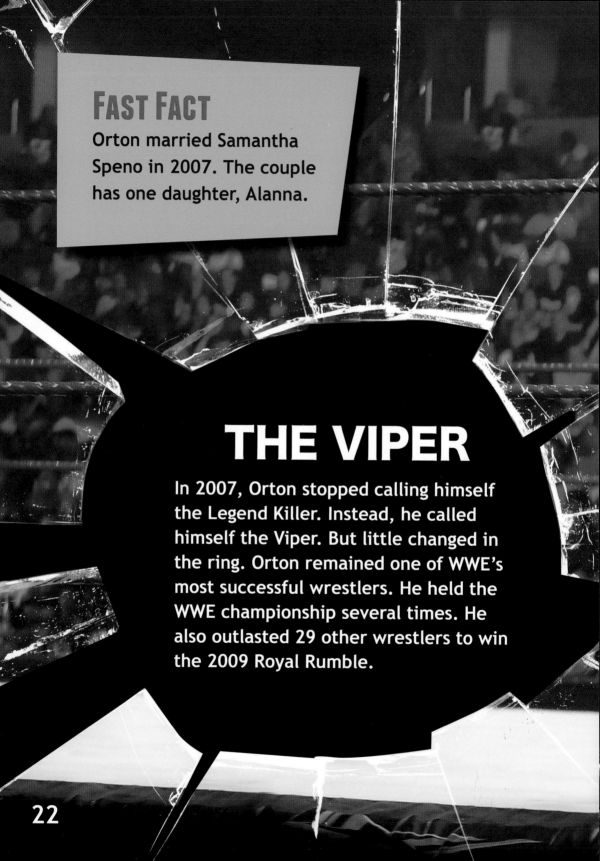

THE VIPER

In 2007, Orton stopped calling himself the Legend Killer. Instead, he called himself the Viper. But little changed in the ring. Orton remained one of WWE's most successful wrestlers. He held the WWE championship several times. He also outlasted 29 other wrestlers to win the 2009 Royal Rumble.

Orton lays a beating
on Primo in 2009.

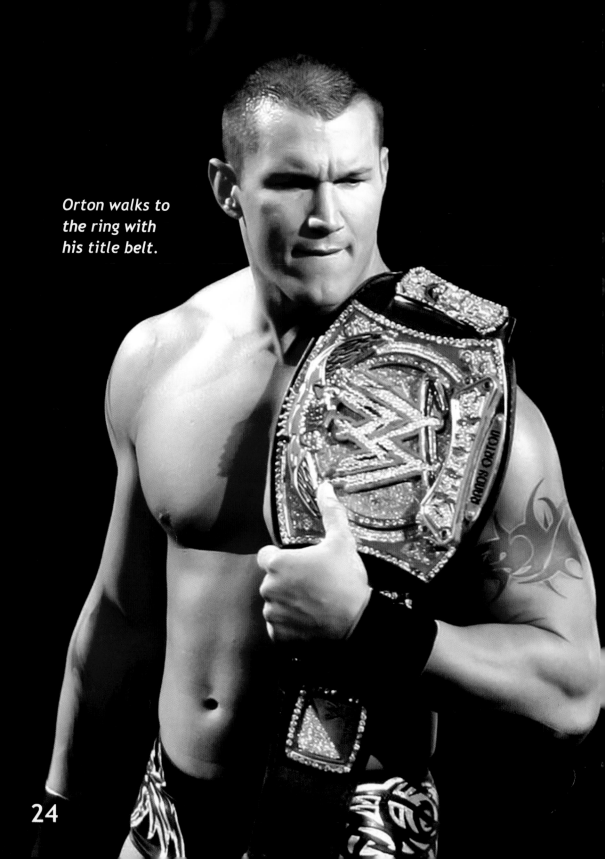

Orton walks to the ring with his title belt.

In 2010, Orton faced five of WWE's biggest stars in the Six-Pack Challenge elimination match. The bout came down to Orton and WWE champ Sheamus. The champ went for his finishing move. But Orton dodged it and hit him with an RKO. He pinned Sheamus to earn his sixth WWE championship.

Orton puts the hurt on CM Punk.

Orton battles CM Punk at WrestleMania 27.

FAST FACT

Orton's character claims to hear voices in his head. His entry music is a song called "Voices."

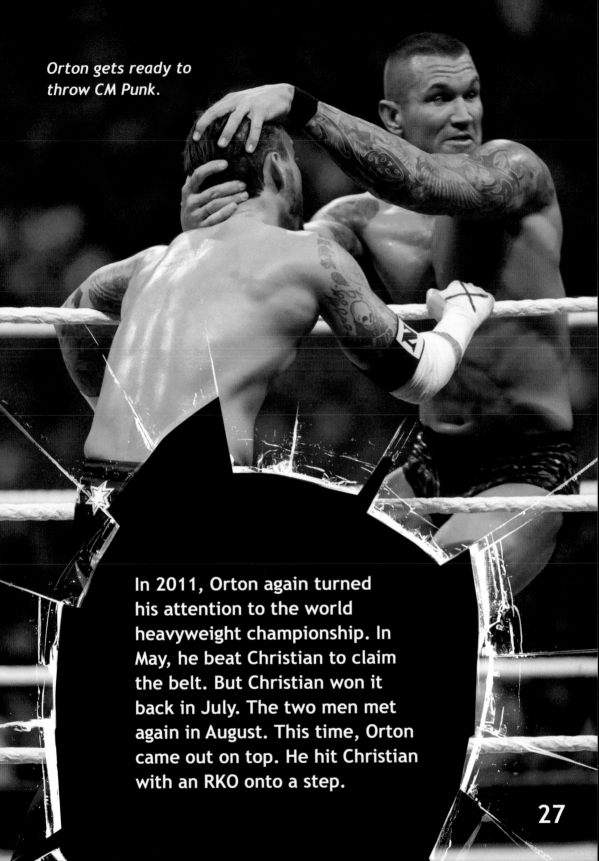

In 2011, Orton again turned his attention to the world heavyweight championship. In May, he beat Christian to claim the belt. But Christian won it back in July. The two men met again in August. This time, Orton came out on top. He hit Christian with an RKO onto a step.

Orton is one of WWE's toughest superstars.

FAST FACT

Orton has held a top belt nine different times. He has won the WWE championship six times and the world heavyweight championship three times.

Orton remains one of the biggest stars in WWE. His size, talent, and skill on a microphone have kept him at the top of WWE for more than a decade. His father is already a member of the WWE Hall of Fame. It's only a matter of time before Randy joins him.

Orton poses for the crowd.

TIMELINE

1980
Randal Keith Orton is born on April 1 in Knoxville, Tennessee.

1998
Orton graduates high school and joins the Marine Corps.

2000
Orton begins wrestling in small, independent leagues.

2001
WWE signs Orton to a developmental contract.

2004
At age 24, Orton becomes the youngest wrestler to hold the world heavyweight belt.

2007
Orton wins his first WWE championship.

2009
Orton outlasts 29 other wrestlers to win the Royal Rumble.

2011
Orton reclaims the world heavyweight championship.

GLOSSARY

baby face
A wrestler whom fans view as a good guy.

developmental contract
An agreement in which a wrestler signs with WWE but wrestles in smaller leagues to gain experience and develop skills.

enlist
To join the military.

finishing move
A powerful move that a wrestler uses to finish off an opponent.

heel
A wrestler whom fans view as a villain.

hardcore
A style of wrestling that disregards traditional rules, such as the ban on foreign objects.

rival
An opponent with whom one has an intense competition.

INDEX